THE STORY OF
NEIL
ARMSTRONG

A Biography Book for New Readers

—— Written by ——
SARAH L. THOMSON

——Illustrated by——
CAN TUĞRUL

ROCKRIDGE
PRESS

D0062820

For all explorers.

Series Designer: Angela Navarra
Interior and Cover Designer: Suzanne LaGasa
Art Producer: Tom Hood
Editor: Orli Zuravicky
Production Editor: Nora Milman

Illustration © Can Tuğrul, 2020;
Photography NASA/Lee Jones, p. 48; World History Archive/Alamy, p. 49; NASA/Alamy, p. 50.

ISBN: Print 978-1-64611-530-3 | eBook 978-1-64611-531-0

R0

CONTENTS

CHAPTER 1

A LEGEND IS BORN

Meet Neil Armstrong

A boy who'd been born on an Ohio farm dreamed of floating above the earth. Night after night, he would hold his breath and rise slowly into the air. Houses and trees and cars grew small beneath him. The boy's name was Neil Armstrong.

Humans have always longed to fly. In 1903, brothers Wilbur and Orville Wright built the first powered airplane. A dream of flight had come true.

People kept dreaming. They dreamed of flying higher than an airplane and leaving Earth behind. In 1969, that dream came true as well. Neil Armstrong left his spacecraft and climbed down a ladder onto the surface of the moon. With one step, he became the first human being to walk on another world . . . and one of the most famous **astronauts** of all time.

If you look up at the moon tonight, remember the first astronaut who walked on it. How did the boy who dreamed of floating through the sky get to the moon? Let's explore how Neil Armstrong made it there!

Neil's America

Neil Armstrong's grandparents lived on a farm near the small town of Wapakoneta, Ohio. Neil was born there on August 5, 1930. It was a difficult time in the United States, a time called the **Great Depression**. Up to a quarter of the people in the country could not find work.

Neil's family was lucky because his father had a steady job. To stay in that job, though, he had to move from town to town. His family

moved along with him. By the time Neil was 14, he had lived in 16 different places. Still, Neil's father brought home a paycheck regularly.

MYTH & FACT

MYTH	FACT
Everyone was poor during the Great Depression.	A lot of people struggled to pay for food or housing, but some had steady jobs. A few were very rich indeed.

Times may have been hard for many, but new ideas and inventions seemed to be everywhere in the 1930s. A lot of families bought their first radios. Superman showed up in comics for the first time in 1938, and Batman came a year later. People were thrilled to try the new ballpoint pens that didn't smudge or need to be filled up with ink! Amazing!

Airplanes had also come a long way in a short time. In 1927, a young pilot named Charles Lindbergh became the first to cross the Atlantic Ocean without stopping. His **solo** trip lasted 33 hours.

Nine years after Lindbergh's flight, Neil got a chance at his first airplane ride.

JUMP —IN THE— THINK TANK

What new inventions of today might seem ordinary or even boring in fifty years?

WHEN?

1903	1929	1930
Wilbur and Orville Wright fly the first airplane.	Great Depression begins.	Neil Armstrong is born on August 5.

CHAPTER 2

THE EARLY
YEARS

Growing Up in Ohio

It was 1936, and Neil's family was living in Warren, Ohio. Neil was five or six years old. He and his father drove past an **airfield** where a pilot was offering rides. Neil's father decided to give flying a try.

Inside the plane were 12 passengers who sat in chairs woven out of wicker. Everything rattled and shook during takeoff. Neil's father was scared. But Neil? He was thrilled. He'd loved planes ever since he got his first toy airplane as a toddler.

When he was a bit older, he discovered model planes. Slowly, Neil pieced together tiny aircraft from wood and tissue paper. He had a little sister, June, born in 1933 when Neil was nearly two. A brother, Dean, came along in 1935. Sometimes Neil would let June or Dean fly one of his planes out a window. But he kept most of his models, hanging them on strings from the ceiling. He wanted to design airplanes when he grew up.

If Neil wasn't making models, he was often reading or working on a Boy Scout badge. He joined a troop in 1941, when he was 11.

That was the year that the United States entered **World War II**. A group of countries

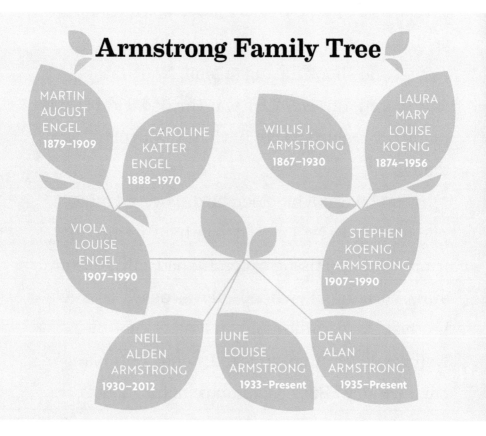

Armstrong Family Tree

MARTIN
AUGUST
ENGEL
1879–1909

CAROLINE
KATTER
ENGEL
1888–1970

WILLIS J.
ARMSTRONG
1867–1930

LAURA
MARY
LOUISE
KOENIG
1874–1956

VIOLA
LOUISE
ENGEL
1907–1990

STEPHEN
KOENIG
ARMSTRONG
1907–1990

NEIL
ALDEN
ARMSTRONG
1930–2012

JUNE
LOUISE
ARMSTRONG
1933–Present

DEAN
ALAN
ARMSTRONG
1935–Present

called the **Allies** were fighting against Germany, Italy, and Japan. The United States became part of the Allies, and the Boy Scouts helped! Neil's troop made model planes for pilots to study so that they could learn the difference between enemy planes and Allied ones.

 Kid Pilot

In 1944, Neil's family moved back to Wapakoneta. Around the time he was 15, Neil decided that he wanted to learn to fly. But first he'd have to make enough money for lessons.

Neil had always earned his own spending money. When he was younger, he mowed lawns at a cemetery for 10 cents an hour and worked at a bakery, where he climbed inside a giant mixing bowl to scrub it clean. Now at 15, he got

a job at a drugstore, doing chores for 40 cents an hour. Flying lessons cost nine dollars an hour . . . so it took more than 20 hours of work to pay for one hour of flying.

 He never did anything wrong. He was **Mr. Goody Two-shoes**, if there ever was one. It was just his nature.

— *Neil's sister,*
JUNE ARMSTRONG

Because Neil was too young to drive, he'd bike or hitchhike out to the airfield. That's where he would climb into an Aeronca Champ for his lessons. On his 16th birthday, August 5, 1946, Neil got his pilot's license. He was thrilled, but a little disappointed, too. He longed to make a record-breaking flight—to be the first to cross an ocean, to fly at the speed of sound, to do *something*.

JUMP —IN THE— THINK TANK

Would you like to set a record? What can you imagine doing that no one else has ever done?

WHERE?

WARREN

INDIANA   OHIO

WAPAKONETA

WEST LAFAYETTE

But it seemed that most records had already been set. Neil felt he'd been born too late.

One year later, Neil left for college at Purdue University in Indiana. He was 17, and his dream had not changed. He still wanted to design airplanes. The first step was to study **engineering**. College was expensive, but Neil won a **scholarship**, an award that would pay for his education if he spent three years in the Navy.

What would he do for the Navy? He'd fly planes.

WHEN?

United States enters World War II.	World War II ends.	Neil earns his pilot's license.	Neil starts college at Purdue University.
1941	**1945**	**1946**	**1946**

CHAPTER 3

AN AMERICAN

HERO

The Navy Years

In 1949, after two years at Purdue University, Neil traveled by train to Pensacola, Florida. He would return to college later to finish his engineering studies. For now he was a **midshipman**, an officer in training in the Navy.

At first, Neil found himself in a classroom, studying the basics. He learned how he was supposed to polish his shoes, who to salute, and how to signal in **Morse code**, a simple code that uses a combination of long and short signals to replace letters of the alphabet.

Before long, Neil was back in the pilot's seat. He flew a North American SNJ, a faster and more powerful plane than anything he'd flown before. He enjoyed the training, even though it was tough. There was no room for mistakes in the Navy.

To complete basic flight training, Neil had to show that he could land on a giant ship called an

aircraft carrier. The runway on a ship is short, and any error could be dangerous. If a pilot were to come in a little too high, too low, too fast, or too slow, he would have to circle around and try again.

Not Neil. He landed on the carrier just right. He'd passed basic training. Now he moved on to advanced training and a new plane, the F8F-1 Bearcat.

In all, Neil's training took a year. Once it was over, he was a **naval aviator**, and he had the badge to prove it—a set of gold wings pinned onto his uniform.

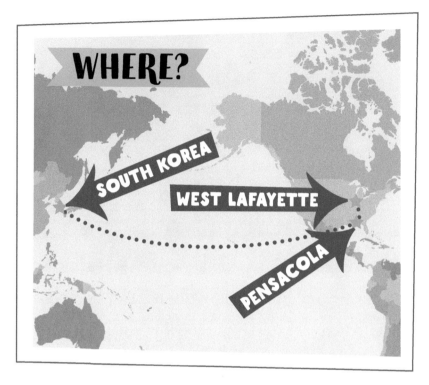

🚀 Fighting for Our Country 🚀

In 1950, the year Neil earned his aviator's wings, war broke out halfway around the world. The country of Korea had been split in half after World War II. The **USSR**, or Union of **Soviet** Socialist Republics, supported the government of the northern half. The United States backed the government in the South.

When soldiers from North Korea invaded the South, the United States decided to help the South fight back. At 20 years old, Neil became part of a group of pilots called **Squadron** VF-51, flying a Grumman F9F-2B fighter jet. His squadron's job was to make it difficult for the North Korean army to get the supplies it needed. On his seventh mission, Neil's plane hit a cable, slicing off about six feet of the right wing. Neil managed to keep the plane in the air, but he knew that he might lose control at any minute. There was no way he could land. His only choice was to bail out. But he was over enemy territory.

> **If I got a little too slow . . . I was going to lose control of the airplane.**

Piloting his plane with care, Neil kept it in the air and managed to get back over safe ground. Then his **ejection seat** sent him flying. His

JUMP
—IN THE—
THINK TANK

What do you think helps someone stay calm in the face of danger?

parachute opened as his damaged plane crashed, and he landed in one piece. His cool head and courage had kept him alive.

In all, Neil flew 78 missions during the Korean War. He returned home in 1952 with an Air Medal for his first 20 combat missions, two Gold Stars, the Korean Service Medal, the Syngman Rhee Medal, and a United Nations Service Medal.

WHEN?

Neil begins flight training for the Navy.	Neil finishes flight training. The Korean War breaks out.	Neil is forced to bail out of his airplane.	Neil returns home from the war.
1949	**1950**	**1951**	**1952**

CHAPTER 4

A PILOT'S LIFE

Time to Soar

Neil went back to Purdue University to continue studying engineering. He met someone who caught his attention—a young woman named Janet Shearon. Neil was 22 and Janet was 18. Neil was quiet and calm. Janet was outgoing and talkative. But their differences did not keep them apart. Neil graduated from college in 1955, and he and Janet got married the next year.

Neil was now an engineer as well as a pilot, and he found a job that let him use both skills. He became a test pilot, helping design and fly brand-new aircraft. It was just what he'd wanted to do when he was a boy carefully creating his models.

In the 1940s and '50s, planes were becoming faster and more powerful than ever. Some could fly faster than the speed of sound, more than 700 miles per hour. Others could carry nearly

200 passengers. Scientists all over the world
were hard at work trying to figure out if it might
be possible to build aircraft that would do more
than soar from place to place on Earth. Could
they actually send human beings into space?

In 1958, the US government created the National **Aeronautics** and Space Administration—**NASA**. NASA's job was to find out if space exploration was possible and how it could be done. Could they build rockets powerful enough to escape Earth's **gravity**? Could they keep living things alive where there was no air to breathe and no gravity to depend on?

Test pilots like Neil were helping find the answers as they pushed their planes to the very edge of space.

California Bound

Neil and Janet moved to California so that Neil could work at Edwards Air Force Base, where the most advanced aircraft were being built. There, in October of 1955, Neil flew faster than the speed of sound in a F-100A jet.

WHERE?

WEST LAFAYETTE

CALIFORNIA

INDIANA

PASADENA

Neil worked for seven years at Edwards, flying more than 900 flights in planes like the North American F-100 Super Sabre, the McDonnell F-101 Voodoo, and the Lockheed F-104 Starfighter. He made seven flights in an experimental plane called the North American X-15, designed to reach the edge of Earth's **atmosphere**.

To fly the X-15, Neil put on a **pressure suit** like the one he would later wear as an astronaut. The suit would protect him as the air around his plane got too thin to breathe. Then Neil's plane was carried up by another aircraft and launched. On his last flight in the X-15, Neil climbed nearly 40 miles above Earth.

During Neil's time at Edwards, he and Janet started a family. In 1957, they had a son, Eric Alan. They called him Ricky. Two years later came a daughter, Karen Anne.

When Karen was two years old, she began to have trouble controlling her eyes. She tripped often. Janet took Karen to the hospital, and doctors found that she had a growth inside

WHEN?

Neil starts work at Edwards Air Force Base.	Neil and Janet get married.	Eric (Ricky) Alan Armstrong is born.
1955	**1956**	**1957**

her brain, a rare kind of brain **tumor**. In 1962, just a month after her third Christmas, Karen passed away.

It was never easy for Neil to talk about his feelings.

66 I thought the best thing for me to do in that situation was to continue with my work, continue things as normal as I could. 99

In his grief for Karen, he threw himself into his work. The year she died, he applied to be an astronaut.

CHAPTER 5
NEIL THE ASTRONAUT

The Space Race

The United States wanted to be the first to reach space. But there was another country that wanted to also—the USSR. Each country was trying to outdo the other. The **Space Race** was on.

At first the USSR seemed to be in the lead. In 1957, the year Neil's oldest son was born, the Soviets launched Sputnik 1 and 2. These two **satellites** were the first spacecraft to **orbit**, or circle, Earth. Sputnik 2 even carried a passenger, a dog named Laika. Sadly, Laika only lived a few hours into her flight, but she showed that living beings could survive in space. The USSR set another record in 1961,

when Yuri Gagarin became the first human being to orbit Earth.

MYTH & FACT

All the astronauts in the early space programs were men.

Russian **cosmonaut** Valentina Tereshkova became the first woman in space in 1963. She orbited Earth 49 times.

A year later, in 1962, NASA sent John Glenn into space. He became the first American in orbit. That was the same year that Neil's daughter, Karen, died. It was also the year that President John F. Kennedy gave a famous speech. He challenged his country to be the first to land an astronaut on the moon.

To meet this challenge, the nation would need new astronauts. NASA had a list of requirements. The new astronauts had to be test pilots who had studied engineering or science.

They had to be US **citizens**. They had to be no older than 35 and no taller than six feet.

Neil Armstrong fit every requirement. He applied and was accepted.

He wasn't sure human beings would ever reach other worlds, but the idea was thrilling. If it was going to happen, he wanted to be a part of it.

Let the Training Begin!

In 1962, Neil, Janet, and their son, Ricky, now five years old, moved to El Lago, Texas. There Neil began his training, along with the other eight astronauts accepted into the space program.

The astronauts practiced putting on pressure suits. They learned how to survive in jungles and deserts in case a spaceship crashed. They climbed into a machine that whirled them in circles on the end of a 50-foot arm. This let them

JUMP
IN THE
THINK
TANK

Would you like to be an astronaut? Which parts of the training sound hard? What sounds fun?

get used to what it would feel like to be in a spaceship going fast enough to blast off from Earth.

The astronauts also spent time in **simulators**. These were copies of spacecraft, where astronauts worked the controls just as they would on a mission. They learned how to handle being **weightless** as well, in a plane that came to be known as the "Vomit Comet."

If a plane soars quickly up and then down, anyone onboard will float for about 30 seconds at the highest point. Neil and the other astronauts seized those 30 seconds to practice the things they'd need do to in space. They glided from wall to wall. They tried eating and drinking. They used wrenches and other tools.

Neil also had to spend time traveling. All the astronauts in training took turns going around the country to give speeches, shake hands, pose for photos, and talk to reporters. Neil was so busy that he sometimes didn't come home until the middle of the night.

During this time, Neil and Janet had another baby, a boy named Mark Stephen. Ricky was an older brother again. And Neil was about to go to space.

WHEN?

USSR launches Sputnik 1 and 2.	Yuri Gagarin orbits Earth.	John Glenn orbits Earth.	Mark Stephen Armstrong is born.
1957	**1961**	**1962**	**1963**

CHAPTER 6

TO THE MOON!

🚀 Neil in Space 🚀

On March 16, 1966, Neil sat in a Gemini spacecraft with another astronaut, Dave Scott. After three and a half years of training, his first space mission was about to start.

Gemini VIII would circle Earth and join up with a target vehicle already in orbit. Two spacecraft **docking** in space would be an important part of any moon mission. Neil and Dave needed to prove it could be done.

After blastoff, the Gemini settled into orbit. Neil brought it closer and closer to the target vehicle waiting there. Finally, at three inches per second, he connected the two spacecraft. They were docked.

Then things started to go wrong.

The Gemini, still connected to the target vehicle, began to tip. Neil and Dave undocked the Gemini, but it started rolling even faster. Dave sent a message to mission control, the people at NASA in charge of the mission. "We have serious problems up here," he said. "We're tumbling end over end up here."

One of the Gemini's **thrusters**, which controlled how the spaceship moved, wasn't working. Neil's vision began to blur. He needed to steady his spacecraft before he and Dave passed out.

To stop the spinning, Neil had to use some of the fuel he'd need to come back to Earth. He and

Dave were forced to make an emergency landing in the Pacific Ocean.

Neil had completed the first docking in space. He'd stayed cool in an emergency, and he'd brought his spaceship home. But he could not celebrate. He felt that he hadn't finished everything he'd set out to do. The mission may not have been a failure, but for Neil, it wasn't truly a success.

Next Stop: The Moon

Neil and his fellow astronauts flew 10 Gemini missions. Now NASA was ready to move on to the Apollo program. Apollo's goal was to meet President Kennedy's challenge and land on the moon before 1970.

> " I think we're going to the moon because it's in the nature of the human being to face challenges. It's by the nature of his deep inner soul. "

The plan was for a rocket to blast off from Earth, carrying a spacecraft that had two **modules**, or parts. The **command module** would take three astronauts from an orbit around Earth to an orbit around the moon. The **lunar module** would bring two of those astronauts the rest of the way to the moon's surface.

JUMP
IN THE
THINK
TANK

What makes someone a good leader?

The rockets, the spacecraft, and the pressure suits that the astronauts would wear all needed to be tested. The Apollo astronauts flew mission after mission to be sure it would all work. Finally, it was time for Apollo 11, the mission that would send three astronauts to the moon.

Michael Collins would pilot the command module. Edwin Aldrin Jr., nicknamed "Buzz," would be the pilot of the lunar module.

The commander of the mission was Neil Armstrong. Cool, quiet, calm, and always focused

on the job, Neil thought more about the mission than about himself. NASA trusted that he could get a spacecraft and its crew safely to the moon and back.

For six months, Neil, Mike, and Buzz trained for 14 hours a day, six days a week. On July 16, 1969, they woke up at 4:15 in the morning. They had 25 minutes for breakfast—steak, eggs, toast, juice, and coffee. Together they headed for the giant Saturn rocket that would launch them into space.

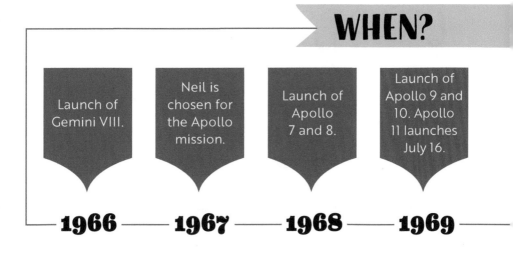

WHEN?

| Launch of Gemini VIII. | Neil is chosen for the Apollo mission. | Launch of Apollo 7 and 8. | Launch of Apollo 9 and 10. Apollo 11 launches July 16. |

1966 —— 1967 —— 1968 —— 1969

CHAPTER 7

ONE STEP FOR A MAN

Men on the Moon

It took three days to reach the moon. Neil, Buzz, and Mike traveled in the command module, *Columbia,* which was docked with the lunar module, *Eagle.* They slept floating in hammocks or above their seats. They sucked their meals from tubes so no crumbs would float around the spacecraft. Neil liked the spaghetti best.

Once they reached the moon, Mike stayed in *Columbia.* Neil and Buzz crawled into *Eagle.* This was the part of the mission Neil was most worried about. The moon's gravity is different from Earth's. Everything there is lighter. No one knew what it would be like to set down a **lander** there.

The landing site was on a steep slope. Neil saw that it wasn't safe. He looked for a better spot as his fuel burned away. At last, with less than a minute of fuel left, Neil took *Eagle* down. It landed so gently he hardly felt a bump.

Neil and Buzz struggled into their space suits. Neil backed out of the hatch and climbed down a ladder onto the moon itself. When he was a boy, Neil had longed to do something no one else had done. Now he'd done it. Millions back on Earth heard his words.

> That's one small step for man, one giant leap for mankind.

Neil planned to say "a man," not "man." Maybe he skipped the "a." Or maybe the radio didn't pick it up.

Neil and Buzz took pictures and collected samples of rocks and soil. They set up a small American flag and a device to measure the distance from Earth to the moon. Then they left a plaque that said, "Here men from the planet Earth set foot upon the moon, July 1969 A.D. We came in peace for all mankind."

🚀 The Man, the Legend 🚀

Neil, Buzz, and Mike returned to Earth and landed safely in the Pacific Ocean. The three astronauts were then taken to Houston, Texas, and kept in **quarantine** for 21 days for their safety. After that, Neil had one quiet day with Janet, Ricky, and Mark. Then there were parades and speeches and interviews, a dinner with the president, and a world tour. All three astronauts received the Medal of Freedom, which is a very high honor.

Neil did not fly any more missions for NASA. In 1971, a year after Apollo 11, he left to become

JUMP
—IN THE—
THINK TANK

Would you like to be famous? What would be good about having everyone know who you are?

a professor at the University of Cincinnati.

Neil and his family moved to Ohio. Neil quit his teaching job in 1979 and took on new work. One of his jobs was making ads for a car company, Chrysler.

Piles of mail came every day, asking for autographs, pictures, or interviews. Neil never enjoyed the attention, but he answered as many letters and gave as many speeches as he could.

In 1989, Neil and Janet decided not to live together any longer. Though he was lonely at first, Neil grew happier when he met Carol

Knight. In 1994, Neil and Janet officially **divorced** and Neil married Carol. They were

together until August 25, 2012, when Neil passed away from heart trouble. It was only a few weeks after his 82nd birthday. Around the world, everyone remembered the war hero who had become an astronaut.

Neil had always known that putting his foot onto the moon was a giant step. But for him it was just a first step. He believed that his mission to the moon proved humans could go anywhere. He was sure that, one day, we'd go deeper into space.

Neil Armstrong would always be known as the man who led the way.

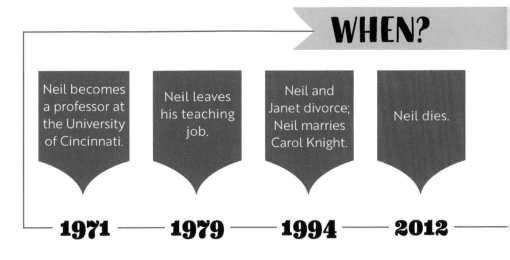

WHEN?

Neil becomes a professor at the University of Cincinnati.	Neil leaves his teaching job.	Neil and Janet divorce; Neil marries Carol Knight.	Neil dies.
1971	**1979**	**1994**	**2012**

CHAPTER 8

SO. . .WHO IS

NEIL
ARMSTRONG

?

Challenge Accepted!

Now that you know so much about Neil's life and work, let's test your knowledge with a little who, what, when, where, why, and how quiz. Feel free to look back in the text to find the answers if you need to, but try to remember first.

1. Where was Neil born?
→ A   Near Cincinnati, Ohio
→ B   Near Houston, Texas
→ C   Near Wapakoneta, Ohio
→ D   Near Tampa, Florida

2. What hobby did Neil have as a boy?
→ A   Collecting stamps
→ B   Playing baseball
→ C   Baking cupcakes
→ D   Building model airplanes

3. **How old was Neil when he got his pilot's license?**

→ A 12
→ B 16
→ C 22
→ D 99

4. **What war did Neil fight in?**

→ A World War II
→ B Gulf War
→ C Korean War
→ D Revolutionary War

5. **What was the mission of Gemini VIII?**

→ A To dock with another spacecraft while in orbit
→ B To fly to the moon
→ C To land in the ocean
→ D To orbit Earth

6.   What record did Neil set?

→ A   Flying the first plane across the Atlantic
        Ocean
→ B   Being the first American in space
→ C   Making the first moon landing
→ D   Flying the most missions in the
        Korean War

7.   Who flew on Apollo 11 with Neil?

→ A   Buzz Aldrin and Michael Collins
→ B   Dave Scott and Frank Borman
→ C   John Glenn and Yuri Gagarin
→ D   Santa Claus and the Easter Bunny

**8.   What was the name of the
       lunar lander?**

→ A   The *Robin*
→ B   The *Hawk*
→ C   The *Chickadee*
→ D   The *Eagle*

9. When did Neil land on the moon?

→ A 1922
→ B 1945
→ C 1969
→ D 1999

10. What did Neil say when he stepped onto the moon?

→ A "That's one big step down from that ladder."
→ B "That's one small step for man, one giant leap for mankind."
→ C "That's one giant step forward in the Space Race."
→ D "Oops, I slipped."

Our World

How did Neil's accomplishments change our world today? Let's look at a few things that have happened because Neil Armstrong took the first steps on the moon.

→ There have been five moon landings since Apollo 11. Apollos 12, 14, 15, 16, and 17 got there safely. Apollo 13 was forced to return to Earth without landing on the moon.

→ NASA is studying how to get humans to Mars. No astronauts have landed on Mars yet, but robotic landers have. Soon NASA hopes to launch a lander named *Perseverance*. A seventh grader from Virginia, Alexander Mather, picked the name.

→ The International Space Station is orbiting Earth right now. Astronauts can live there for months at a time.

→ Some inventions for space travel end up being used on Earth. Here are some things you might see every day that were first developed for the space program: cameras in smart phones, ear thermometers, wireless headsets, and the computer mouse.

JUMP IN THE THINK TANK FOR MORE!

Now let's think a little more about the things that Neil did, the ways he changed our world, and how those changes might affect the future.

→ Is it important to explore space? Why?

→ It took three days for Apollo 11 to reach the moon. It would take months for astronauts to reach Mars. What would be hardest about such a long trip?

→ Think about these qualities: courage, loyalty, intelligence, calmness, curiosity, kindness, toughness, gentleness, responsibility, the ability to think quickly. Which do you think are most important for an astronaut?

Glossary

aeronautics: The science of how objects (like airplanes) travel through the air

aircraft carrier: A large ship used by the military to get troops and planes where they are needed. A carrier has a deck long enough for planes to take off and land.

airfield: A field where airplanes can take off and land

allies: Countries that fight together against an enemy

astronaut: A human being who travels into space

atmosphere: The gases (such as oxygen and nitrogen) that surround a planet

citizen: A person who legally belongs to a country or place

command module: The part of the Apollo spacecraft where the crew stayed during the flight to the moon

cosmonaut: A Soviet or Russian astronaut

divorced: No longer married

docking: Bringing a ship or a spacecraft together with something else (usually either a dock or another ship or spacecraft)

ejection seat: A device that can fling a pilot free from an aircraft in an emergency

engineering: The use of science to design and build items that humans can use, including machines, tools, buildings, airplanes, and spacecraft

gravity: The force that pulls two objects toward each other. It keeps you on the ground and causes objects to fall.

Great Depression: A period of time in history during which people had little money to spend, work was scarce, and many businesses failed. It lasted from 1929 until the late 1930s and affected countries all over the world.

lander: A spaceship that sets down on the surface of a planet or a moon

lunar module: The part of the Apollo spacecraft designed to carry two astronauts from orbit around the moon to the moon's surface

midshipman: An officer in training in the Navy

module: Part of a spacecraft that can be connected to others or used on its own

Morse code: A code that uses dots (short signals) and dashes (long signals) to replace letters of the alphabet. Morse code can be sent using flashes of light or bursts of sound. The most famous piece of Morse code is three dots, three dashes, and three dots. It stands for SOS and is a signal for help.

NASA: The National Aeronautics and Space Administration, an agency of the US Government. NASA oversees space exploration and research.

naval aviator: A pilot for the US Navy, Marine Corps, or Coast Guard

orbit: To circle around a planet, star, or other object

pressure suit: A suit worn by pilots or astronauts to protect them and allow them to breathe when there is little or no pressure, or force pushing down, on the body from the air outside. A full-pressure suit, or a space suit, works where there is no air at all. A partial pressure suit works when the air is very thin.

quarantine: Keeping someone away from other people for a period of time to make sure they aren't sick and don't get others sick

satellite: Something that orbits a planet, star, or other object

scholarship: An award that pays for a student to attend school

simulator: A machine that is an exact copy of the controls used to fly a vehicle such as a spacecraft. A pilot can be trained to fly on a simulator, which allows him or her to make mistakes without being harmed.

solo: Alone

Soviet: Part of the Union of Soviet Socialist Republics, or USSR

Space Race: A competition between the US and the USSR to see which country could put astronauts into space first. The USSR seemed to be ahead, but they did not succeed at making a manned moon landing.

squadron: A group of pilots under a single commanding officer

thruster: Part of a spaceship or boat that controls how it moves

tumor: A lump or growth inside the body. Some tumors are harmless, but others may be very serious.

USSR: Union of Soviet Socialist Republics, also known as the Soviet Union. A country that existed in Eurasia from 1922 until 1991, when it broke into several separate countries, including Russia, Lithuania, Belarus, Armenia, and Ukraine

weightless: The state of floating free from gravity

World War II: A war that took place in Europe from 1940 to 1945. The Allies—countries including Great Britain, the United States, France, and the USSR—banded together to fight the Axis countries, which included Germany, Italy, and Japan.

Bibliography

BBC News. "10 Key Moments in Space Exploration." Published Jan. 15, 2016. BBC.com/news/science-environment-35326827.

Hansen, James R. *First Man: The Life of Neil A. Armstrong.* New York: Simon & Schuster, 2005.

History.com. "History Stories: Life for the Average Family During the Great Depression." Updated August 31, 2018. Accessed 1/14/20. History.com/news /life-for-the-average-family-during-the-great-depression.

JPL Infographics, NASA. "20 Things We Wouldn't Have Without Space Travel." Accessed February 26, 2020. JPL.NASA.gov/infographics /infographic.view.php?id=11358.

Meltzer, Brad, and Christopher Eliopoulos, ill. *I Am Neil Armstrong.* New York: Dial Books for Young Readers, 2018.

NASA. "Apollo Missions." Accessed February 5, 2020. NASA.gov/specials /apollo50th/missions.html.

NASA. "The Red Planet." Accessed February 26, 2020. Mars.NASA.gov /#red_planet/5.

Wegener, Leon. *One Giant Leap: Neil Armstrong's Stellar American Journey.* New York: Forge, 2004.

Wolverton, Mark. "The G Machine." *Air and Space Magazine.* Published May 2007. AirSpaceMag.com/history-of-flight/the-g-machine-16799374 /?page=1.

About the Author

Sarah L. Thomson has published more than 30 books, including prose and poetry, fiction and nonfiction, picture books and novels. Her work includes two adventures featuring a teenage girl ninja, poetry for picture book readers, and nonfiction about gorillas, sharks, plesiosaurs, saber-toothed cats, and other fascinating creatures. *School Library Journal* called her picture book *Cub's Big World* "a big must-have."

Sarah worked as an editor at HarperCollins and Simon & Schuster before becoming a full-time writer. She lives in Portland, Maine. Learn more about her work at SarahLThomson.com.

About the Illustrator

Can Tuğrul / Illustrator of childrens books / collector of old medals / protector of street cats / traveler of flea markets / passenger of night trains / owner of the last cookies / addict of postcards / watcher of sci-fi movies / lover of long journeys. Can currently lives in Istanbul and is always drawing something.

WHO WILL INSPIRE YOU NEXT?

EXPLORE A WORLD OF HEROES AND ROLE MODELS IN
THE STORY OF... BIOGRAPHY SERIES FOR NEW READERS.

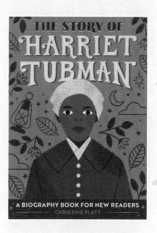

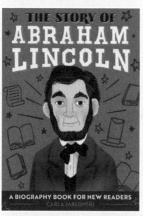

LOOK FOR THIS SERIES
WHEREVER BOOKS AND EBOOKS ARE SOLD

Alexander Hamilton	Jane Goodall
Albert Einstein	Barack Obama
Martin Luther King Jr.	Helen Keller
George Washington	Marie Curie